INSPIRATIONAL
FOOTBALL
STORIES

FOR YOUNG READERS

12 Extraordinary Tales of Football Legends
and Astonishing Plays to Inspire
Kids to Greatness
+ 100+ Amazing Fun Football Facts

MICHELLE WEISS

CONTENTS

INTRODUCTION

There is no other game like American football. Something amazing happens when the big lights come on, and the clock starts ticking. Those everyday people who run onto the field become like superheroes, pushing their bodies and minds to the limit to do the impossible. Defensive players plow through strong offensive lines. Quarterbacks throw halfway down the 100-yard field. Receivers catch the ball using only their fingertips.

No two football games are exactly alike. With different players, fields, and even weather, each game is a new chance for something amazing to happen. Maybe a quarterback's pass will bounce off another player's shoulder and land in a teammate's arms. The losing team could make an amazing comeback in the fourth quarter.

Football has a long history of amazing plays and players. Since the first football game in 1869, great men have flocked to football because it's where everyone is pushed to do their very best—and maybe even more. Think of Joe Montana, who was backed into a corner and threw a pass that became legendary.

Anthony Muñoz was injured time and again but kept coming back and wowing fans. Tom Brady barely made it into his first pro season but pushed himself to become the "greatest of all time" quarterback.

In this book, you'll find just a few of the hundreds of inspiring stories that make up the history of the NFL. Each of the legends you'll read about wasn't just an amazing athlete but a person with strengths and weaknesses, just like you. They came from different backgrounds and faced challenges, but they had two things in common—they loved football and were determined to give their best in every game they played.

With each player comes a unique story of how they overcame the obstacles in their life. You can have a story just like them. Whether you're an athlete, a fan, or barely know anything about football, there is a story here. The athletes you'll read about weren't just good at football. Some were calm under pressure. Others could beat the odds no matter what. While reading about their amazing abilities, you might discover some of your own.

Even though these men might be legends now, they were once kids just like you. They faced challenges as they grew up. They made mistakes and learned from them. As you read through their stories, you won't just learn about amazing plays. You'll see how qualities like courage, perseverance, and determination separate the good men from the great ones.

So get ready, turn the page, and learn the true strengths behind some of the greatest athletes to ever walk the field.

TOM BRADY:
FROM UNDERDOG TO GOAT

Tom Brady, the Patriots legend. More Super Bowl wins, quarterback wins, Super Bowl MVPs, and Pro Bowl picks than any other football player. He's known as the greatest of all time (GOAT). When you say "football," he's the first player many football fans think of. He's broken almost every record possible for a quarterback in the NFL and then some.

But before all of that, he was overlooked time and again.

TOM OVERLOOKED

Tom started playing football and baseball when he was just a kid. By the time he got through high school, he was known for his amazing ability in both sports—but not by everyone. When he sent out recordings of his football games, hoping to get a scholarship, the responses were not hopeful. One recruiter said, "Thanks for sending us your tape, but it doesn't look like your skill set fits our offense." No one wanted him on their team.

Baseball was a different story; Tom got an offer to be on a pro team right out of high school. But, as much as he loved baseball, his heart was with football. He turned down the baseball offer and accepted a football scholarship to the University of Michigan, one of the only schools interested enough to send a recruiter. It seemed like someone finally appreciated his football abilities.

But it didn't last. When Tom arrived at the Wolverine team at the University of Michigan, he found that two of the three coaches who had picked him for the team had left the school. The new coaches didn't care much about him. He was benched and hardly played during his first two years on the team. This was a tough time for Tom, and he struggled with feeling sad, angry, and worried about his future. He loved football and knew he was a good player, but his coaches weren't giving him the chance to show what he could do. Tom wanted to transfer to a different college, but one of his coaches talked with him and said, "Just put everything else out of your mind and worry about making yourself better."

WHO'S THE QUARTERBACK?

Tom decided to stop wasting his energy complaining and do something about his situation. He met with the college's assistant athletic director, Greg Harden, every week to learn how to improve. He realized that part of his problem was his size; everyone thought he was too skinny for a quarterback. He practiced harder than ever and eventually got on the field. He became the starting quarterback in 1998, but his troubles weren't over.

In 1999, his final year in college, Tom's position as a starter was challenged by Drew Henson, who was a year younger than Tom. Unlike Tom, Drew was wanted by everyone. He was considered "the best high school QB to ever come out of the state of Michigan" and was personally recruited. But Tom was older and more experienced and knew the position belonged to him. He was willing to prove it, too.

Coach Carr of the Wolverines set up an interesting way to solve the issue. In every game, he had Tom play in the first quarter and Drew in the second. Whoever played better would play the entire second half of the game. Tom won the spot in the first four out of five games, but after games six and seven were a disaster, Coach Carr made Tom the starting quarterback again.

Tom was the king of comebacks and last-minute wins in college, leading the Wolverines to victory repeatedly, even when it seemed hopeless. During the years he played, he scored 20 wins and five losses and ranked high in the Wolverines' records for yards, touchdown passes, and more.

NUMBER 199

Tom was excited about his successes in college after fighting for a starting spot for so long, but once again, he faced challenges. Tom watched the NFL draft on TV with his family, expecting to be picked in the second or third round of players. But one, two, three, four, five rounds went by. Tom hadn't been picked. He and his family sat in shock. Tom was embarrassed and wondered if he would be picked at all. In those few minutes, he saw his future changing. What would he do if he couldn't play pro football?

This was one of the most challenging moments in Tom's life. Can you imagine sitting there, watching the TV, and wondering if you would be picked to do the one thing you had trained to do your whole life?

Tom was so embarrassed that he left his family so he could be alone. Eventually, he discovered he was drafted in the sixth round, the 199th player picked overall, and the seventh quarterback chosen by the New England Patriots. While he wasn't the very last one picked, he was almost last, and Tom remembered the draft as a difficult time in his life for the rest of his career. Many years later, he cried while talking about the draft in an interview.

Even though Tom did eventually get picked, the fact that he was the seventh Patriots quarterback didn't look good. He remembered sitting on the bench for two years in college and was worried that it would be the same again.

A PATRIOT

Although Tom sat on the bench again in his rookie season, he played more than he did in college. By the end of his first season, he worked his way up from seventh to second quarterback. And by 2001, his second season, he was the Patriots' starting quarterback.

Even now that he had his pro starting spot, things weren't as easy as he'd hoped. He didn't play his best as a starter in the first few games but continued to work hard. For example, Tom worked personally with a strength coach named Mike Woicik to increase his speed and strength. He also talked to the older members of his team and learned tips from them. Most of all, Tom "treated every practice like it was a game." He was serious about getting better.

Tom did so well that he led his team to the Super Bowl in 2001. Everyone feels nervous before a big match, and it shows in different ways like pacing, sleep problems, shaking hands and feet, and more. These are all the normal signs you would expect Tom to show before his first Super Bowl game, but he didn't. Instead, Tom took a nap in the locker room.

Rested up, Tom did well in the game, but the Patriots were struggling. With just one minute and 29 seconds remaining, the game was tied. Most thought it would be best for the Patriots to wait for the timer to run out and try to win in overtime.

But Tom had different ideas. He set the stage for an incredible nine-play drive that put the Patriots in position for a field goal. The kick went straight through the goalposts, and the Patriots beat the Rams with only a few seconds remaining. The stadium exploded with cheers; the Patriots had just won their first Super Bowl. Tom Brady was named MVP and set a new record as the youngest quarterback to win a Super Bowl at 24.

BECOMING THE GOAT

Tom Brady had his ups and downs throughout the rest of his career, but he always tried his best in every practice and game. He broke too many records to count, but some of his most famous records are related to the Super Bowl. He still holds 11 Super Bowl records, including wins, appearances, completions, and touchdown passes. Some of his records are related to his age, right when he started and before he retired. He became the youngest player to win the Super Bowl, but later became the oldest player ever to be voted Super Bowl MVP at 40.

Tom never forgot how difficult it was to become the greatest quarterback—and one of the greatest players—the NFL has ever seen. While working hard to train himself in his first years with the Patriots, he developed the TB12 method, a lifestyle for young and old athletes to help them stay strong and in shape. "This regime is one that I want all athletes of all ages to experience, and the principles that fuel the peak performance I've enjoyed over the years are, I believe, also the future of sports training," Tom said. TB12 does include a way to exercise, but it also helps athletes learn how to train their muscles and eat well so that their body stays in good condition. Through TB12, Tom hoped to help young athletes struggling like he was when he was in high school and college.

Tom Brady's career started with many disappointments. Even though he was a good player, his coaches and teammates didn't see how great he could become. So, Tom decided to train hard. He reached out for help, worked with his coaches and teammates, and slowly got stronger until he became the Patriots' star quarterback.

It hurts when people don't recognize our talents, but Tom Brady didn't let that stop him, and you don't have to, either! Keep working hard and never give up on the things you love to do. Remember to reach out for help when you need it and help others when they need you. Maybe one day, everyone will talk about your underdog story as much as Tom Brady's.

THE STEEL CURTAIN:
THE POWER OF TEAMWORK

THE START OF THE STEELERS

From the year it formed in 1933, the Pittsburgh Steelers seemed destined to have bad luck. Before 1970, when the National Football League (NFL) was created, the Steelers only qualified for playoffs once and lost the game with no points on the board. One season, they didn't win any games at all. The only thing the Steelers were known for was player Byron White, who would later become a Supreme Court justice. Byron only played with the Steelers for one year before transferring to the Detroit Lions.

Other NFL teams weren't worried about going up against the Steelers. Pittsburgh simply couldn't get the right players to make a good team. To make things even worse, in 1970, the Steelers moved to a new stadium and were hit with a $3 million relocation fee. How were they supposed to sign good players after spending all that money?

Everything changed when the Steelers hired a new coach, Chuck Noll. He was so good at picking amazing athletes that within five years, he selected ten players who would go on to be inducted into the Pro Football Hall of Fame. Now, those were some smart picks. It's rare for a team to pick two or more future Hall of Famers in one year, but Noll's record was five in a single draft. It remains the record today.

Chuck Noll's carefully picked players kicked off what's known as the "Steelers dynasty" of football in the 1970s. For the first time, the Steelers became well-known in the NFL and would make history within ten years.

THE STEEL CURTAIN

The backbone of the Steelers' winning years in the 1970s was called the "Steel Curtain." This referred to the team's defense that was so powerful it turned the Steelers' losing streak around. While many players were part of this defensive team, four main players led the Steel Curtain to victory.

First was "Mean" Joe Greene, who got his nickname from how powerful he was on the field. He became known as the most important player in the Steel Curtain. L.C. Greenwood, or "Hollywood Bags," was known for his dream of being an actor and the gold shoes he wore on the field. Ernie Holmes was a fierce player who eventually became a wrestler and actor. Finally, "Mad Dog" Dwight White became famous for leading the Steelers to their first Super Bowl championship. He was sick in the hospital the week before the game, and no one expected him to play. However, he attended the game and immediately gave his team an opening to score.

These four men were all quite different. They came from different homes, states, and colleges. They were drafted in two different years. But, despite their differences, they came together and worked hard to make their team great; that's the true power of teamwork. Without them, the Steelers might still be a losing team today.

These four men didn't just change the Steelers, though. They changed the way everyone looked at football. Most people were focused on the offensive line and didn't think much about the defense players. The offense players get the ball down the field, score touchdowns, and take charge of the plays, so they gain more attention. NFL teams were looking out for good offense and overlooked great defensive players.

Even today, people sometimes overlook the importance of defense. However, the Steel Curtain proved that a good defense is just as valuable as a good offense. Stopping the opposing team from getting the ball down the field—the defensive line's job—is an effective way to win a game. It's not all about scoring touchdowns.

ZEROES TO HEROES

Joe, L.C., Ernie, and Dwight, along with the rest of their defensive line, led the Steelers to many victories. Throughout the '70s, the Steelers made the playoffs eight times. They became the first team to win more than two Super Bowls and still hold the record for winning four Super Bowls within six years.

In 1976, the Steelers' Steel Curtain was possibly the best football defense in history, but the season started disappointingly. After winning the Super Bowl in 1975 and

1976, the team was excited for the '76 season in the fall. However, they began with one win and four losses. In the fifth game, the Steelers' quarterback, Terry Bradshaw, got hurt and was out for the rest of the season. It was starting to look like the Steelers' glory days were over.

But the Steel Curtain wasn't going to give up. The Steelers' defense put their heads together and decided they wouldn't let their team go down. There were nine games left in the season, and in eight of them, the Steel Curtain didn't allow a single touchdown to get past them. If that wasn't amazing enough, the opposing team didn't score a point in five of those games, called a "shutout." Over the season, an average of 3.1 points per game got past the Steel Curtain, and the Steelers won by an average of 22 points.

No one had seen a defense like that before, and no one has seen one since. It showed the world that individual talent doesn't matter as much as working together. The four leaders of the Steel Curtain took the Steelers from a bad season start to one of the most memorable seasons in the NFL. It didn't matter that the Steelers didn't make it to the Super Bowl that year; hardly anyone remembers the Raiders winning the title. They do remember the Steelers' famous defense, which they admired so much that they were nicknamed the "Steel Curtain." Eight of the eleven starting defense players in the Steel Curtain were picked for the Pro Bowl in 1976, and four of them, including Joe Greene, eventually made it into the Pro Football Hall of Fame.

TEAMWORK WORKS

Even though Joe Greene was the most famous member of the Steel Curtain, he couldn't have played such a legendary season alone. He needed help from the other defensive players to make it happen. Nothing is stronger than many people working together toward one goal. Teamwork is one of the most powerful things we can use, but it's not always easy. Every person is unique, so to work toward one goal, we must put aside differences. We also must let each person use their strengths and admit our weaknesses.

The Steel Curtain proved that you can achieve anything with teamwork, confidence, and perseverance. So the next time you find you can't do something alone, try asking for help. The Pittsburgh Steelers' Steel Curtain shows us that when people work together, nothing is impossible.

PEYTON MANNING:
NEVER THE EASY WAY

Every football player wants to make a name for themselves. They hope that after they retire, they'll leave a legacy that people will discuss for years to come. For Peyton Manning, this was never an easy goal. Most players start with a clean slate, but Peyton was born with expectations to live up to. He would have to prove his skill to make his mark on the world, as his dad was the famous New Orleans quarterback Archie Manning.

Because Peyton's dad was so well-known, Peyton was almost guaranteed a football career. He could have received a football scholarship without trying too hard, but he decided from an early age that he wanted to take the more challenging road so he could prove himself—and he certainly did.

A FOOTBALL FAMILY

Peyton grew up playing football. While Archie Manning played for the New Orleans Saints, Peyton and his brothers interacted with pro football players from a young age and enjoyed tossing a ball around with them. However, Peyton and his brothers chose to play football; their dad never forced them to. Archie's rule was that if his sons wanted to play football, they had to come to him. Archie wanted his sons to pursue their dreams, but it so happened that all their dreams revolved around football.

Peyton, especially, loved football. He didn't rely on his dad to teach him things; he sought out every chance to learn more about the game. From a young age, he was excited to watch his dad's games from the stands. He even watched tapes of his dad's old college games. He knew everyone his dad had played with and could list almost every play he'd seen. Peyton had a talent for remembering details, which would help him throughout his football career.

After studying football so much, Peyton was ready to play the game. He went to high school at Isidore Newman and played so well on his team that in his 10th-grade year, he was chosen as the starter quarterback. Peyton's older brother Cooper was also on the team as a wide receiver. The two brothers became known as an unstoppable force, and that year, their team made it to the Class 2A semifinals. Cooper graduated that year and went to Ole Miss, where his dad went to college, but because of his health, he had to stop playing football. Peyton supported his older brother and wore his #18 jersey while still in high school to honor him; #18 would become Peyton's number for the rest of his football career.

Peyton played well throughout high school and won a Player of the Year award before graduating. Every college wanted him to play on their team, and Peyton had a tough decision to make. The obvious choice was to go to Ole Miss, his dad and brother's college. But, in a move that shocked everyone, Peyton chose to attend the University of Tennessee. This was so unexpected that Ole Miss fans sent Peyton's parents angry letters; they all wanted to see Peyton on the team that made his dad famous.

But Peyton stuck with his decision, and his parents supported him, so he was off to Tennessee. Later, Peyton said he chose Tennessee because he didn't want to go down the easiest path. He knew he was already popular at Ole Miss and would receive special treatment because of his family. He wanted to go somewhere where he had to work hard and prove himself. Being comfortable at Ole Miss wouldn't help him grow into a better football player, but the challenges awaiting him at Tennessee would.

MAKING HIS PLAYS

Throughout his four years with the University of Tennessee Volunteers, Peyton's performance did not disappoint. Before his first season was over, he was named the starting quarterback and remained in that position until he graduated. He became the greatest passer in Volunteer history with 89 touchdowns and 11,201 yards. He also broke the Southeastern Conference record for career wins, winning 39 of the 45 games he played as a starting quarterback.

Peyton completed his college degree in three years, and with such a fantastic record, everyone expected him to go straight to the NFL draft. He was already one of the top picks, if not *the* top pick. Instead, Peyton did the unexpected: he stayed to play for his senior year at Tennessee. Once again, Peyton saw a chance to challenge himself and gain more experience. It paid off, as Peyton was able to rack up an amazing record his senior year and became an even more popular pick for the NFL draft.

Peyton knew that the Indianapolis Colts were looking for a quarterback like him, but he was up against another rookie quarterback named Ryan Leaf. While Ryan had a better rating, most people thought Peyton's performance was better. What made the Colts notice Peyton was the maturity he'd gained from his last year in college. The Colts scheduled a meeting with Ryan and Peyton before the draft, and while Peyton showed up professionally and on time, Ryan was late.

When it was time for the 1998 NFL Draft, the Colts picked Peyton first. They were so confident in their choice that they traded their starting quarterback to get Peyton and paid him more than most rookies. This put a lot of pressure on the Colts and Peyton. If Peyton didn't do well, the team would look bad.

The start of Peyton's first season with the Colts was rough as he adjusted to a new team, but by the end of the season, he set multiple rookie records, including most interceptions and touchdown passes. While it took the Colts a few years to earn any major titles, Peyton led them to the playoffs multiple times and set them on a winning streak.

OFF THE FIELD

Peyton Manning is known as one of the best NFL quarterbacks ever, but being a good football player wasn't his only goal. He wanted to make the world a better place by helping people in need, and often, he used football to do it. It would have been easy for Peyton to live his comfortable life as a famous football player without caring about anyone else, but instead, he used his time, money, and talents to give back to the community.

Even though Peyton challenged himself whenever possible, he recognized that becoming a pro football player was easier because of his dad. He knew that many kids with great talent might not make it to the NFL simply because they didn't have the right people to train them, and he didn't want that to happen. So, Peyton and his wife Ashley created the Peyback Foundation to help young kids and give them the opportunities they needed to be successful. The foundation has provided over $15 million to support its cause, allowing kids nationwide to live their dreams.

Peyton has also donated generously to hospitals over the years and has a children's hospital named after him. When powerful Hurricane Katrina swept through New Orleans in 2005, Peyton and his brother Eli were quick to help the people hit by the storm and donate to help rebuild the city.

The entire Manning family helps the community yearly through the Manning Passing Academy, a summer camp where football players can practice their skills. Archie, Cooper, Peyton, and Eli Manning run the summer camp together, bringing in coaches and famous football players nationwide to train young athletes.

Peyton won many awards throughout his incredible pro career. Still, the one that meant most to him was the Byron "Whizzer" White Humanitarian Award, named for a former NFL player who loved giving back to the community. Peyton was named the winner in 2005, saying, "I am truly humbled by this honor. This means a lot to me because what I do off the field is much more important than anything I do on the field."

It took a lot of extra work in the offseason to run the Peyback Foundation and the Manning Passing Academy. But it was worth it to show Peyton how much he loved his community.

THE LAST TRIAL

After 14 seasons with the Colts, including many playoff games, Super Bowl appearances, one Super Bowl championship, and MVP wins, Peyton had neck surgery in 2011 that kept him from playing that season. It became clear how important he was to the team because the Colts lost 14 games.

After the surgery, Peyton had to relearn how to play football. At first, something as simple as throwing the ball was hard for him. Many people doubted if he would return to football. He could have given up rather than taking months to relearn the most basic movements, but Peyton didn't take the easy path. He kept training to play the game he loved and eventually could get on the field again.

However, his recovery had taken a long time, and the Colts were hurting after many losses. To the surprise of many fans, Peyton's beloved team let him go. Once again, Peyton could retire, and many expected it. But he was determined to leave a fantastic legacy and show the world he could still play. So, Peyton signed on with the Denver Broncos for the 2012 season and did so well that he was named NFL Comeback Player of the Year. He gave the Broncos success they hadn't had in many years, leading them to several playoff games and winning a Super Bowl championship in his final season.

TAKE THE CHALLENGING PATH

After 18 successful years of pro football, it's no wonder that Peyton Manning was ushered into the Pro Football Hall of Fame in 2021. He was such an obvious choice that the group who made the decision took only 13 seconds to approve. Peyton didn't get to the Hall of Fame by doing what everyone else did; instead, he kept choosing the more difficult path that strengthened him.

Many times, it's tempting to take the easiest path in life, but the easy way is never the most rewarding. By challenging himself both on and off the field, Peyton earned too many awards, honors, and records to count. More than that, he could use what he'd gained to give to others in need. The more you challenge yourself and grow stronger, the more you can help those around you.

Take the harder path sometimes, just like Peyton Manning did. It might not be easy, but you will be thankful for it in the end.

PATRICK MAHOMES:
MAKING THE IMPOSSIBLE POSSIBLE

No other athlete has redefined the game of football like Patrick Mahomes. He's undoubtedly a good quarterback; he can throw far, run quickly, and easily dodge the opposing team's offense. What sets Patrick apart, however, are his incredible passes that no one is prepared for. Usually, before a game, both teams study how the opposing team plays to be ready for what will happen.

This doesn't work with Patrick. His moves are so different in every game that the only thing you can count on is that he'll be outstanding. He's amazed fans, teammates, and opposing teams as he's taken the Chiefs from an average team to a powerhouse no one wants to face.

But what exactly makes Patrick such an incredible threat to any opposing team?

PATRICK'S SECRET

Though Patrick's quick and unique passes look like luck, they result from many hours of practice. Patrick learned early that he didn't play football like everyone else. Instead of trying to be like the other athletes on his teams, he embraced himself and brought his personality into his playing style. His ability to think creatively and make quick, confident decisions helped him create new passing methods perfected with a lot of hard work.

Patrick always had a strong arm, but that wasn't all he could do. Once he combined his natural strength with flexibility from baseball, he did things that no one had seen on the football field. Sometimes, he looked like a pitcher when he threw the football. Other times, he did a quick flick of the wrist, and the ball was gone. Sometimes, he didn't look where he was throwing and executed the throw flawlessly or threw with his non-dominant left hand. Patrick could throw from almost any angle, giving him an advantage on the field. Many said he "played the quarterback position unlike anyone who had come before him."

This creativity is also one of the reasons why Patrick enjoyed playing football so much. His enthusiasm shined in every game he played. In most pictures, he wears a huge smile. For some pro players, football becomes a routine. But Patrick continued to play with joy and childlike wonder every time. He saw every game as a chance to do something new. This happiness also contributed to his strength and dedication in every game he played.

To Patrick, playing pro football meant he got to live his boyhood dream every day.

THROWING TOO FAR

Patrick was born with a great throwing arm, which doesn't come as a surprise since his dad was a pro baseball player. Patrick grew up around his dad's teammates and was taught how to pitch, pass, and run by some of the best athletes in the country. More important than any skill, he discovered his love for sports. From an early age, he showed great promise as a baseball and football player.

Patrick often practiced throwing in the backyard with his dad as a boy. Though their yard was large enough for a pro baseball player, Patrick soon threw balls over the fence and into the neighbor's yard. Patrick's dad eventually found a baseball pitch where Patrick had more room to practice his unique moves, but even that wasn't enough. Patrick could throw from the plate over the 220-foot-high sign at the other end of the field. Finally, Patrick's dad brought him to a football field where he could practice his throws safely. As Patrick got older, though, his high school coaches worried about him hitting the opposing punter on the far side of the field.

Like most great football players, Patrick played many sports, but he most enjoyed football and baseball. He could pitch a 93-mile-per-hour ball and had one of Texas's best high school batting records. In football, he was just as skilled. In his senior season as starting quarterback, he made 50 touchdowns, rushed almost 1,000 yards, and threw for 4,619 yards.

With that kind of record, it's no wonder the Detroit Tigers pro baseball team drafted Patrick after graduation. Only a few colleges offered him a football scholarship because they weren't sure about his commitment to football. It seemed like the obvious choice to play baseball, especially since his dad had played for 11 seasons.

But Patrick wanted to do things his way. Since he loved both sports, he accepted a football scholarship to Texas Tech University, where he could also play baseball. Eventually, he followed his heart again and gave up baseball for football. It was a good thing, too, as he became one of the leading college passers in the country within two years.

GOING PRO

Everyone wanted him by the time Patrick got to the NFL Draft of 2017. He was the tenth pick in the first round, selected by the Kansas City Chiefs. Patrick was encouraged by the Chiefs' manager, who called him "one of the best players I've ever seen," but his rookie season didn't go as planned. He played backup to starting quarterback Alex Smith and barely saw any action in his first season.

Patrick could have gotten disappointed and angry. He was one of the NFL's best incoming players, and it seemed unfair that he didn't get to play right away. But Patrick kept a smile on his face and his head held high. The following season, Alex Smith was traded, and Patrick became the Chiefs' starter for the 2018 season.

Patrick did not disappoint. His enthusiasm and unusual passes worked so well that in his first season as a starter, he became the second quarterback in history to throw for 5000 yards and score 50 touchdowns in one season. Peyton Manning was the first quarterback to meet such a record, but he did it in his sixteenth season. Patrick did it in his *second.* Already, everyone knew he would become one of the greatest quarterbacks of all time.

Patrick's performance was so impressive that he led the Chiefs to a record season of 12-4, took his team to the AFC Championship Game, and was voted NFL MVP at only 23. Though the Chiefs lost that year, it wasn't a massive blow to the team. They knew if Patrick could do something like that in his first season as a starter, their winning streak was only beginning.

They were right. The following year, Patrick brought his team to the Super Bowl. Patrick struggled in the first half of the game but turned it around in the fourth quarter to win his team the title. He was voted Super Bowl MVP, the youngest player ever honored. Patrick led the Chiefs to another Super Bowl victory in 2022 and was again named Super Bowl MVP. At the time of writing, Patrick had led the Chiefs to the playoffs in all six years he'd been with them.

THE BEST GAMES

While Patrick's plays are unique in every game, a few games stand out as memorable in his career.

Kansas City Chiefs vs. Pittsburgh Steelers—2018

This game was in Week 2 of Patrick's first season as a starter. Everyone was already impressed by how he'd gone up against the Los Angeles Chargers the week before, but he outdid himself against the Steelers. He achieved six touchdowns with 326 passing yards and earned the highest passer rating of his career.

Kansas City Chiefs vs. Baltimore Ravens—2019

This was an important game for the Chiefs. It was the first home game of the season, and they had already won their first two away games. After Patrick's outstanding 2018 season, the Chiefs were eager to keep their record spotless in 2019.

The Ravens weren't going to go down easily. Their defense was one of the best in the NFL that year. The Chiefs were nervous, but Patrick wasn't. He went into that game like he always did, smiling as he played the game he loved. He easily took down the Ravens' defense with a completed 27 out of 37 passes, 374 yards, three touchdowns, and no interceptions. The Chiefs won the game 33-28.

Kansas City Chiefs vs. New York Jets—2020

Even though everyone expected the Chiefs to win this game, no one predicted how thoroughly Patrick would stomp the Jets and escape their defense. He didn't turn over the ball or get sacked once throughout the game, all while making five touchdowns and 416 passing yards.

JUST BE YOU

In his sixth season with the Chiefs, Patrick shows no signs of stopping his awe-inspiring career soon; he already holds four NFL records and many honors and awards. There's no doubt that however long Patrick plays for the NFL, he'll continue to lead his team to victory and exceed expectations time and again.

While Patrick is dedicated, works hard, and knows the value of teamwork, his true greatness comes from the unique personality he brings to the field. His wacky passes have redefined what's possible for a quarterback. But he would have never become a legend if he had done the same thing as everyone else.

What makes you unique? We all have our talents and personalities. Embracing who you are and using your strengths wisely can lead to amazing things, just like with Patrick Mahomes. It's okay to do things your way, even if it's a little different from everyone else. All you must do is just be you!

THE MINNESOTA VIKINGS 2022 COMEBACK: A WINNING ATTITUDE

AN UNCERTAIN GAME

The start of the 2022 season was uncertain for the Minnesota Vikings. The year 2021 was not good for them; they lost nine games and won eight. Their manager and coach were fired because of all the losses. With a new coach and manager and a losing streak behind them, the Vikings didn't know what was in store for the 2022 season.

Under their new coach, the team racked up an eight-win-one-loss record, the best they'd had in over ten years. One of those wins was against the Buffalo Bills, a close game many thought was the best NFL game of the season. However, not many thought the Vikings would make it to the playoffs. Most of their wins were close, and most of their losses were huge. This odd points average caused the Vikings to have more lost points than gained points over the entire season, even though they won 13 games and lost four.

Going into Week 15, the Vikings were nervous. This game against the Indianapolis Colts would decide who won the NFC North title and entered the playoffs. Fans were nervous, too. Both the Colts and the Vikings had been struggling in recent seasons, so no one knew who was more likely to win the game.

The Vikings' nerves got the better of them at the start of the game. The Colts kept pushing down to the end zone, and even though the Vikings' defense kept them back for a while, they soon lost their hold. The Colts scored enough field goals and touchdowns to earn 33 points in the first two quarters. Meanwhile, the Vikings hadn't scored once.

"FIVE MORE TOUCHDOWNS"

The Vikings players weren't doing well during halftime. They were angry and frustrated that they'd let so many points get past them, and they knew that the Colts were already the winners. No NFL team had ever gone from zero to 33 points in the second half of a game.

But cornerback Patrick Peterson didn't look at what hadn't been done before. He looked ahead at what his team could do. "You just need five touchdowns. That's nothing," he told the offense. Kirk Cousins, the Vikings quarterback, didn't think he was serious. How could they possibly win when they were 33 points down?

But once Coach Kevin O'Connell encouraged his team after Patrick's words, the Vikings made a decision. Even if they couldn't win the game, they would do their best in the second half. They recognized that they made many mistakes in the first two quarters and promised not to make the same mistakes again.

As a team, the Vikings decided to have a winning attitude, even when they were losing. They got back out onto the field with their heads held high.

THE SECOND HALF

At first, it didn't seem like anything changed. The two teams fought for the ball in the first several minutes of the third quarter but didn't get anywhere. The Colts decided they no longer needed to score since they were ahead by so many points. All they had to do was keep the Vikings from scoring, and for a while, they did just that.

There's something in football called "win probability." All it means is that people try to guess who will win the game while it's still happening. Since the Colts had a 33-point lead, everyone was sure that they would win the game. Kirk Cousins finally scored a touchdown for the Vikings; still, everyone knew the Colts would win. One touchdown was nothing.

But the Vikings saw one touchdown as one of the five they needed. One touchdown meant they were on their way to winning.

Even when the Colts scored a field goal, the Vikings didn't give up. They pushed down the field and scored another touchdown. Everyone still expected the Colts to win, but they were less certain.

When the fourth quarter began, things changed. Justin Jefferson of the Vikings caught a 20-yard pass, then a 17-yard pass. His third catch was a touchdown, bringing the score to

36-21. Inspired by all they had done, the Vikings kept going and scored another touchdown with just over five minutes left. They got another touchdown with a two-point conversion immediately afterward before the Colts could do anything about it.

This brought the game to a tied score of 36-36 with two minutes left on the clock. The crowd in the U.S. Bank Stadium went wild as the game passed into overtime. The Vikings had gone from zero to 36 points within the second half of the game. Before the fourth quarter was over, the win probability experts began to predict that the Vikings, not the Colts, would win the game.

OVERTIME

Overtime was so intense that no one could guess if the Colts or Vikings would win. Both teams gained some ground, but no one scored. Play after play went by. The ball was passed back and forth, but players couldn't make it very far down the field before they were tackled.

At this point, the Vikings could have let their fear get the best of them like they had at the beginning of the game. Instead, each player remembered Patrick Peterson's words: "Just five more touchdowns." They kept up their winning attitude, and something amazing happened.

With 20 seconds left, the Vikings were on the Colts' 27-yard line. There wasn't enough time to score a touchdown, so Vikings kicker Greg Joseph would have to go for a field goal to win. The Colts used a timeout to try to throw Greg off his game, but soon, the players were back on the field with only a few seconds left on the board.

A hush fell over the stadium. Fans all around the country sat on the edge of their seats. The Vikings had already done the impossible by tying the score, but could they win?

The play began. Greg lined up the kick. The ball soared through the air. People began to whisper hopefully. The whispers turned into shouts as the ball flew closer to the goalposts. Score!

The stadium exploded with cheers. Greg's teammates crowded around him, lifted him, and shook him excitedly. The team grinned and tried to catch their breath. The Vikings had just won the NFC North title and were going to the playoffs. However, they had done more than that. The Vikings had just completed the greatest comeback in NFL history, going from zero to 39 points in the second half of the game.

THE GREATEST COMEBACK

It wasn't luck that helped the Vikings make their incredible comeback. Even though winning looked impossible, Patrick Peterson believed they could do it. He convinced the rest of his team to believe, too. Together, they chose to go into the second half of the game with a winning attitude, even if they did lose. They all pulled together, admitted their mistakes in the first half of the game, and promised to do better in the second half. Every player did their best, from the amazing defensive line to Greg Joseph, who kicked the winning field goal.

It's hard when you realize that you're losing. If you find yourself far from your goal, like the Vikings, it may feel impossible to get ahead. But the Vikings understood that they would lose only if they gave up. They could be proud of themselves even if they lost the game if they did their best and gave it everything they had in the second half. With this winning attitude, the Vikings won.

Never give up, even if it looks like you'll lose. The best thing you can do is start every day with a winning attitude and give it your all. You never know what amazing things might happen when you do.

3 FREE GIFTS

Are you enjoying the stories? Hope you are! To make the experience even better, here are 3 Extras that I hope you'll really like:

- Football Activity Book
- Audiobook: Inspirational Football Stories for Young Readers
- Fiction Football Story

Scan the QR Code if you want to have even more fun.

JOHN ELWAY:
LEADING ON AND OFF THE FIELD

When you look at John Elway's records, you'll notice they are surprisingly average for an athlete known as one of the greatest quarterbacks of all time. He's won more games than any other quarterback in the NFL and is known as one of the Denver Broncos' all-time best players. So how did he get such a reputation without breaking many records like the other famous quarterbacks?

In football, a quarterback is the leader of the team. They look out for their teammates rather than trying to boost their stats. John was a good athlete, but his ability to lead his team made him exceptional. He cared about doing his best not to boost his record but to inspire his teammates to give their all. Because of John's dedication to his position, he and his team were able to turn around many games to gain unlikely victories. Through every injury, bad season, and unexpected turn, John led his team with his head held high.

But John didn't become a leader overnight. He had to learn and grow just like everyone else, and it all started with lessons learned from his dad.

THE YOUNG LEADER

John's dad was a football coach and former college quarterback. This meant that John moved around a lot as a kid but didn't mind as long as he could play ball. Wherever he ended up, John found a team and played—and he often became known as one of the best in the group.

His dad encouraged his love of football and taught him all the basics at an early age. As an adult, he would reflect on his time with his dad and realize he set the first leadership example. John didn't know it then, but he wasn't just learning *what* his dad taught him; he was also learning *how* he was teaching him. John's dad taught him it was important always to do your best as a leader to inspire those following you. This dedication was what made John so famous later in life.

By the time John was in sixth grade, he was ready to play on a football team. In his first game, he made six touchdowns in the first half. Because John's dad taught him how to run and pass, John was known as a "dual-threat quarterback." He could easily run with the ball and dodge opposing players when needed.

WHICH SPORT?

Even though John's dad wanted him to be a football player, John's baseball abilities impressed people the most. In his senior year, his team won the Los Angeles City championship, and he was the Southern California player of the year. John loved baseball and football, so he was conflicted when the

Kansas City Royals baseball team drafted him after high school. Ultimately, John turned them down and accepted a football scholarship to Stanford University, where he could also play baseball.

When John first arrived at Stanford, everyone expected him to be a backup quarterback for three years before he was made starter his senior year. This was how other recent quarterbacks had grown on the Stanford Cardinals team. But John walked in with the attitude of a leader and took practices seriously before the season started. He played so well that two other backup quarterbacks transferred to different schools because they knew they wouldn't get to play with John on the team.

They were probably right. While John played as a backup in his first year, he became the starting quarterback in his sophomore year. Stanford never had a winning streak, as John was still working on his team leadership, but John did make a name for himself with an impressive personal record. He threw 27 touchdown passes in his first starting year and 20 in his second. Over his four college seasons, he had 9349 yards, 77 touchdowns, 39 interceptions, and 774 passes. His college performance was so excellent that in 2000, he was inducted into the College Football Hall of Fame.

John wasn't done with baseball, either. He continued to play throughout college and was drafted by the New York Yankees in 1982. He played with them that summer, and many thought he would stay there instead of going into the 1983 NFL Draft.

But John was confident in his decision to pursue football. He was one of the top-rated quarterbacks in the 1983 draft, but getting picked didn't go as he'd planned.

FROM COLTS TO BRONCOS

When football players are drafted, they usually stick with their team for a while before being traded or retiring. But when John was the first quarterback the Colts selected in the first draft round, he wasn't satisfied. The Colts were struggling, and their coach didn't have a good reputation. John wanted to play football but would not play with the Colts. He considered returning to the Yankees to play baseball if he couldn't be traded.

Eventually, John was traded to the Denver Broncos. Football fans across the country knew his reputation and were excited to see him play. John had great stats from college, but everyone wanted to know if he had what it takes to lead a team to victory.

At first, John didn't. While he had learned a lot about leadership from his dad and his sports teams in school, he was still discovering how to put it all into practice. In his first season, John played starter a few times, but veteran quarterback Steve DeBerg often took over to win the games. Steve was named the Broncos' starting quarterback but was soon injured, and John took his place. John finally started to prove himself as he led his team to the playoffs, which the Broncos had only made three times before.

In the years that followed, John would become known as one of the best team leaders the NFL had ever seen. He stood out because he brought his best to every game and encouraged his team to do the same. But in 1986, his fourth season with the Broncos, he made his mark on history at the AFC Championship.

"THE DRIVE"

One of John's greatest moments on the field was "The Drive," a series of offensive plays in the championship game against the Cleveland Browns. The game was close from the beginning, with both teams scoring back and forth. By the end of the third quarter, the Broncos were winning with a score of 13-10. But the Browns pulled ahead to make the score 20-13, and the fourth quarter was more than halfway gone. There was enough time for the Broncos to score, but they had a problem: they were on the opposite end of the field.

It seemed impossible to get down the 100-yard field to make a touchdown before the end of the game. But John brought his team together and told them they could do it. Then they got to work. With John in the lead, they pressed down the field for 15 plays. As they got close to the end zone, John tried to throw two touchdown passes that both fell short. Then, at the five-yard line, John finally threw true. The Broncos made a touchdown and tied the score 20-20 with 37 seconds left in the game. They had just pushed 98 yards in five minutes. In overtime, they scored a field goal that won the game and took them to the Super Bowl.

Without John's leadership, the Broncos would have never made that touchdown. But because he believed in what they could do and performed his best, John led his team to an amazing victory that made NFL history.

MOVING TO MANAGEMENT

John led his team so well that he gave the Broncos victory at the Super Bowl two consecutive years and was named Super Bowl MVP in 1998. The following year, in 1999, John finally decided to retire. However, he wasn't done with football or leading football teams.

John formed an Arena Football League team called the Colorado Crush. It became clear that John was just as good at leading from the sidelines because the team won the Arena Bowl Championship in their third season.

In 2011, John returned to the Broncos not as a player but as their manager. He first signed Peyton Manning, which proved to be one of the best decisions the Broncos ever made. The team immediately won four division titles, two AFC Championships, and one Super Bowl. That became John's third Super Bowl win with the Broncos. Even when John wasn't on the field, the team felt the impact of his dedication and precise choices.

LEADING WELL

If John Elway had stood alone and relied on his abilities, he probably wouldn't have made it far in pro football. But by being confident and rallying his team, John led the Broncos to amazing feats like "The Drive" and their Super Bowl wins.

Who looks up to you as a leader? Maybe it's a friend, sibling, or teammate. Being a leader is a great opportunity to encourage and inspire others. When you work together with your team, there's no telling what you can accomplish. The best part is that when a good leader like John Elway succeeds, their teammates succeed, too. You can be that kind of leader; all it takes is a bit of practice.

J. J. WATT:
THE "NOBODY" WHO LIVED
LIKE A "SOMEBODY"

BIG-TIME DREAMING

J. J. Watt—or "JJ" as most people call him—had a crazy dream as a boy: he wanted to play football. Nothing would be better than to say he was a star player for his hometown college team, the Wisconsin Badgers.

JJ just had one problem. As a kid, he was short and skinny, and football players were supposed to be tall and strong. When JJ told others about his dream, they said it would never come true. They didn't think a scrawny kid like him could become a football player.

Having his dreams laughed at hurt JJ, but his dad taught him to believe in himself, even when no one else did. Every day before school, JJ's dad would gather JJ and his two younger brothers to tell them one simple thing: "Act like somebody." To JJ, this meant that he always tried to do the right thing. He decided to love who he was and never try to be someone else. Most of all, he believed in himself, chased after his dreams, and created his path in life.

Even though JJ still believed in his football dream, for a while, he was more dedicated to ice hockey. He started playing when he was three and traveled all over the world with his team. He enjoyed it, but his heart always went back to football, and he played whenever possible. As he grew into a teenager, he struggled to choose between what his heart told him and what people told him. He was still seen as too small to play football, but he knew it was where he belonged.

So, when he was thirteen, JJ quit ice hockey. He dedicated himself to sports in high school, even though he was smaller than most of the other boys. You might wonder how he could be involved in baseball, basketball, track and field, *and* football when he didn't have an athlete's body. JJ wasn't born with a body for football, but he decided to train his body to become big and strong; it was the only way he could keep up with his teammates.

Remembering his dad's inspiring phrase to always "Act like somebody," JJ designed a workout routine to get his body in shape to play the sports he loved, especially football. Instead of sleeping in like everyone else, he woke up at 4:30—can you imagine that!—and started working out at 5:00 a.m. He did it almost every day, and eventually, his body *did* get stronger. He didn't just keep up with his teammates; he became an all-star athlete. In his senior year, JJ had 399 receiving yards, 26 catches, and five touchdowns as a defensive lineman. He was also given multiple awards and named his team's MVP.

It turned out that with a lot of hard work, JJ *could* play football, after all—but there was still a long way to go before he reached his dream.

COLLEGE CHOICES

Even though JJ played well on his high school football team, college coaches didn't think he was special. Once again, people focused so much on JJ's smaller size that they missed his big heart and dedication to football.

When athletes go to college, they typically need a scholarship that gives them a spot on the college sports team and pays for their college courses. JJ's dream college, the University of Wisconsin-Madison, didn't offer him a scholarship because they didn't think he was a good enough player. He couldn't pay for college, so he decided to go to Central Michigan University, where he was given a scholarship.

After JJ's first year on the team, his coaches tried to tell him that he needed to play offense instead of defense. Defensive players were supposed to be big, so no one could get past them. Strong but still skinny, JJ didn't look like he was right for defense.

Once again, JJ followed his heart and chased his dreams. He knew where he belonged: on defense, playing for the Wisconsin Badgers. So, he left Michigan and transferred to Wisconsin like he'd always wanted.

Even though he would finally live his dream, it wasn't an easy choice. By leaving Central Michigan, he also left his scholarship and starting spot behind. That meant he started at Wisconsin with almost nothing, although he did get to be on the football team. With no scholarship to pay for his courses, he had to find another way to pay for college.

JJ didn't let this obstacle stand in his way—not when he was so close to what he'd always dreamed of. Just like when he was in high school, waking up at 4:30 a.m. to work out, JJ knew that to get to where he needed to be, he had to work harder than everyone else. So, he worked as a pizza delivery boy to help pay for his courses so he could stay at Wisconsin and play football. He worked whenever he wasn't on the field or in a classroom. He had a busy schedule, but it was worth it because he was finally living his dream.

JJ's coaches didn't take long to realize how well he could play. Throughout his college years, he won several awards and recognitions for his impressive record of tackles and interceptions and was once again voted his team's MVP. He did so well that, eventually, Wisconsin gave him a football scholarship—that meant no more pizza deliveries!

NFL DRAFT

In 2011, JJ was drafted by the Houston Texans. He was the first defensive end to be picked, which might sound great, but the Texans' choice was met with boos from their fans. It wasn't a very encouraging start to his pro career, but JJ remembered when people doubted him. He had repeatedly proved them wrong, so he knew he would do it again.

And he did! Those "booers" would soon change their minds. While the Texans had never qualified for the playoffs before drafting JJ, during his ten years playing with the team, the Texans qualified six times, including in JJ's first season. He started his career with a bang, winning multiple rookie honors for outstanding plays. In 2012, he did even better, making his season one of the best of any NFL defensive player ever.

JJ proved himself to be a great football player throughout his ten seasons with the Texans. He became known as one of the best edge rushers ever to take the field, holding a record of 101 sacks, 172 tackles for loss, and 25 forced fumbles. His record is so impressive that he is eligible for the Pro Football Hall of Fame.

BEST GAMES

Usually, football players have one game or play that stands out among the rest. But with J. J. Watt, it isn't possible to single out one game better than the rest because he had so many incredible victories! JJ gave his best in every game, living the words that his dad often told him.

Texans vs. Baltimore Ravens—January 2012

This was the game where those who had booed JJ cheered him instead. While JJ had a good season up until this game, this was the one where he showed what he could do. The Ravens won the game, but the Texans realized they had won something much better: an all-star player in J. J. Watt. He ended the game with 12 tackles and 2.5 sacks.

Texans vs. Oakland Raiders—September 2014

JJ wasn't done surprising people. Almost as soon as the game started, JJ scored a touchdown that made history. It was the first time a defensive player from the Texans scored a touchdown from scrimmage (the beginning of a play).

Texans vs. New York Giants—September 2018

This was a significant game for JJ. In 2016, JJ only played three games because he hurt his back. He returned the following season, but after five games, he had a leg injury and had to sit out for the rest of the season. The Texans weren't doing so well because JJ couldn't play. Some people thought that JJ would never be able to return to his team because of his injuries.

JJ wasn't at his best in the first two games of 2018, but the third game against the New York Giants was different. With his body healed, JJ got back into the game's rhythm. Ultimately, he had eight tackles, three sacks, and a forced fumble. Even though the Giants barely won the game, the overall success set the Texans on a nine-game winning streak, earning them the NFC South title at the end of the season.

Texans vs. Buffalo Bills—January 2020

Once again, JJ got injured in the 2019 season and was placed on the injured/reserve list. He returned at the start of 2020 to be in this playoff game against the Bills. While his one sack, one tackle for loss, and two quarterback hits might not seem as impressive as his previous records, his plays won the game. The Bills were winning 13-0 when JJ sacked their quarterback. This set the Bills back and allowed the Texans to win in overtime with a score of 22-19. Because of this game and another great season, his teammates voted him 45th on the NFL Top 100 Players of 2020 list.

In 2021, JJ finally left the Texans after ten years. His teammates once again voted him into the NFL Top 100 Players of 2021, and he went to play for the Arizona Cardinals.

HEALTH CHALLENGES

After many people doubted JJ, he lived his dream and became a legendary football player. He overcame every obstacle— including his health. He could have quit after getting injured the first time, but instead, he let his body heal and kept going. It happened repeatedly, but JJ didn't let himself be beaten down. He would continue chasing his dream as long as he could.

In 2022, JJ hurt his leg again, and no one was sure if he'd be able to play in the fourth game of the season against the Carolina Panthers. But then, something even worse happened. On a Wednesday, JJ's heart started beating in an odd rhythm. He went to the hospital on Thursday, where the doctors were able to get his heart beating normally again. After that, he could have taken a rest; no one expected him to play right after being in the hospital.

But on Friday, JJ was practicing with his team the day after he visited the hospital. That weekend, JJ was on the field playing against the Panthers.

AGAINST THE ODDS

J. J. Watt faced all sorts of obstacles to playing football. At first, nobody thought he was big or strong enough to do it. Then, nobody thought he was good enough. Even his own health kept him from playing sometimes.

But no matter what came his way, JJ remembered to "Act like somebody." He didn't let anyone tell him how his life would be. Instead, he made his dream happen by working hard and staying dedicated. Even when his body was injured, JJ got back up as soon as possible and kept playing the game he loved. He didn't let anything stop him from doing his] best in every game.

Have you ever faced obstacles to chasing after your dreams? The story of J. J. Watt shows us that it's possible to make our paths, even if it takes extra work. You just have to believe in yourself and remember to own every day of your life.

Act like somebody. Just like JJ, you'll find that your dreams are much closer than you think.

JOE MONTANA:
STAYING COOL UNDER PRESSURE

Unlike most legendary football players, Joe "Cool" Montana's fame didn't come from his strength or size. It didn't even come from how far he could throw. Instead, Joe Montana's strongest abilities were on the inside.

Joe earned his nickname "Joe Cool" early in his career, not because he was destined to be one of the coolest football players of all time but because he stayed calm under pressure. At the end of a game, when things looked bad for his team, Joe didn't panic or let someone else take over. He let his body do the work it had been trained to do while he kept his mind calm and analyzed the field so he could make the best move.

Throughout Joe's high school, college, and pro career, he repeatedly proved that staying "cool" during a game is one of the most important qualities a football player can have. Even though he didn't have the usual build for a quarterback, he became one of the greatest NFL players of all time because he could focus when the clock was running low, and his team was losing hope. In these moments, Joe made confident decisions that often led his team to victory.

"THE CATCH"

The most famous example of Joe's peace under pressure is one of the best plays in NFL history called "The Catch." Joe and the San Francisco 49ers were up against the Dallas Cowboys, one of the most powerful teams in the NFL. The teams were evenly matched, with many wins and few losses throughout the season. However, the Cowboys were expected to win this NFC Championship Game because of their success in previous seasons.

It was 1982, Joe's third season with the team and his first as a starting quarterback. The 49ers were nervous about going up against a team as good as the Cowboys, but Joe didn't let fear stop him from starting strong. He threw a touchdown at the beginning of the game, but unfortunately, the Cowboys immediately came back with a field goal and a touchdown. Joe threw another touchdown pass after one of his passes was intercepted in the second quarter. But once again, the Cowboys responded with a touchdown. They seemed to stay one step ahead of the 49ers throughout the game.

The third quarter was full of uncertainties. First, the Cowboys got an interception from the 49ers, but then the 49ers intercepted and scored another touchdown. The Cowboys again followed on their heels and scored a field goal and touchdown. One of Joe's throws was intercepted again, and the 49ers didn't get the ball back until the fourth quarter. Only four minutes and 54 seconds were left in the game, and the Cowboys led with a score of 27-21.

The 49ers had 89 yards between them and the end zone. Joe slowly but steadily passed the ball down the field to his teammates. Finally, they made it close to the end zone. Joe tried for a touchdown pass but missed his teammate. The 49ers called a timeout to plan one last play for the championship title and a shot at the Super Bowl.

The plan was for Joe to make a pass to wide receiver Freddie Solomon immediately; the same play scored the 49ers a touchdown earlier in the game. Dwight Clark was in charge of keeping the Cowboys away from Freddie, and he was also the backup receiver if Freddie was unavailable.

As soon as the play began, there was a problem. Freddie slipped as he ran to his spot. That meant Dwight was no longer in the right place to defend Freddie from the Cowboys. The Cowboys crowded Freddie, making it impossible for Joe to throw to him. Meanwhile, the Cowboys' defensive line plowed through the 49ers' offense and tried to push Joe out of bounds.

Joe was out of options. His receivers weren't open, and he only had a few seconds before he was pushed out of bounds or tackled by the Cowboys. But Joe didn't lose his calm. Instead, he looked around the field and made a confident decision. He threw a high pass toward the back of the end zone using all his strength. He wasn't sure if anyone would catch it, but if the ball went out of bounds, the 49ers might have another chance to score in the next play. As Joe made the throw, he was tackled, so he didn't see what happened next. Neither did the 49ers' coach, who was anxiously planning how they would win the game after what he thought was a throwaway pass.

But the crowd saw what happened. Dwight stood at the back of the end zone, and though he was covered by one of the Cowboys, he made a considerable leap and grabbed the ball with his fingertips, landing within inches of the field's edge.

When the crowd went wild, Joe knew something had happened. He got up and was amazed to see Dwight with the ball. Together, they had just tied the game with 51 seconds left. The 49ers kicker Ray Wersching scored an extra point, giving the 49ers the lead.

With 51 seconds on the board, the Cowboys tried to run down the field and almost came in range of a field goal, but the 49ers stopped them. The clock ran out, and the 49ers won against all the odds.

"The Catch" instantly became famous for many reasons. It was the defining moment of Joe Montana's career, and it was only his first season as a starting quarterback. This win against the Cowboys also took the 49ers to the Super Bowl, where they won against the Cincinnati Bengals. It was the 49ers' first Super Bowl win, and Joe led them right to it.

But Joe wasn't simply born with his remarkable ability to stay calm. Long before he made it to the NFL, he had to practice like everyone else.

WHERE JOE GOT HIS COOL

Joe loved sports from his earliest years. His dad wanted to inspire and help his son as much as possible, so he always played football with him. Joe's dad soon knew that Joe was a natural athlete and wanted to get him on a team. So, even though Joe couldn't play until he was nine, his dad lied about his age, which got him on a team one year early.

Joe enjoyed football and baseball, but his greatest love was basketball. His dad even created a local basketball team so Joe would have other kids to play with. Soon enough, Joe realized he loved being in the middle of a game. After practicing hard, his body knew exactly what to do, even under pressure. He didn't get nervous because he knew he had put in all the hard work necessary to do his best. In Joe's case, practice did make perfect.

In high school, Joe's athletic abilities got him onto the baseball, basketball, and football teams. At first, he didn't get along well with his football coach because he missed a lot of training while playing other sports. However, in his junior year, his coach made him a starting quarterback, and he held the position until he graduated.

Even though he was successful as a quarterback, Joe still loved basketball the most. In 1973, he even led his team to a championship title. North Carolina State offered him a basketball scholarship, and they told him he could play basketball and baseball while he was there. However, Joe decided accepting a football scholarship to Notre Dame was the right thing to do. He loved the Notre Dame Fighting Irish team since he was a boy.

THE COMEBACK KID

Joe's ability to stay calm under pressure also earned him the nickname "the Comeback Kid" in college because of how many times he was able to turn a game around in the last few minutes. Throughout his 16 years in the NFL, Joe had 31 fourth-quarter comebacks in addition to the comebacks from high school and college. These are just a few of the most amazing ones.

Ringgold Rams vs. Monessen Greyhounds

Joe didn't become a starting quarterback until the third game of his junior year in high school. His team faced Monessen High, one of the school's greatest rivals. Everyone knew that the Monessen Greyhounds would win. They had always been a successful team while the Rams struggled.

They continued to struggle for the first half of the game. With nothing to lose, the Rams' coach replaced the current starting quarterback with Joe after halftime. Joe must have been surprised to be thrown in the game on such short notice, but he didn't show it. The "Comeback Kid" made his name known by making four touchdowns, bringing the score to a tie at 34-34. They might not have won, but everyone was shocked that the Rams had tied such a good team. Joe's performance was so impressive that he grabbed the attention of Notre Dame recruiters, who would eventually offer him a scholarship.

Notre Dame Fighting Irish vs. North Carolina Tar Heels

Joe upheld his reputation when he got to Notre Dame. He didn't get to play much his first year, but during this game in the 1975 season, Joe's focus and determination once again surprised everyone.

Joe was put on the field with five minutes and 11 seconds left. North Carolina led with a score of 14-6, meaning that Notre Dame had to make more than one touchdown to win. That didn't have Joe worried as he calmly stepped onto the field. He was only in the game for one minute and two seconds, but he achieved 129 passing yards and paved the way for a 21-14 victory.

San Francisco 49ers vs. New Orleans Saints

When Joe joined the 49ers, everyone wondered if he was a good pick. He played as a backup in the 1979 season and only threw 23 passes, even though he was in all 16 games.

The 49ers continued to struggle in 1980. Their record would be six wins and ten losses by the end of the season, but they weren't doing as badly as the Saints, who lost all thirteen games they played before the match with the 49ers. Everyone expected the 49ers to win, but it didn't look good initially.

This was one of Joe's first games as the starting quarterback, and while he stayed collected during the game, he was still adjusting to his position. At halftime, the Saints had a 28-point lead, but the 49ers made two touchdowns during the third quarter and brought the score to 35-21. It seemed like a long shot for the 49ers to complete two touchdowns in the fourth quarter. However, Joe Montana brought his legendary calm focus to the game and pushed his team to new heights.

With Joe's amazing performance under pressure, he tied the score at the end of the fourth quarter and allowed his team's kicker to make the winning field goal in overtime. It was the first of many comebacks during Joe's professional career. Even though the 49ers didn't end the season with a great record, it was the last time the team would have less than ten wins in many years. Joe led his team to such amazing wins over the next ten years that the NFL refers to the 80s as the 49ers' dynasty.

A "COOL" LEGACY

Joe inspired teammates, fans, and coaches alike throughout his career. He won four Super Bowls for the 49ers and was voted Super Bowl MVP three times. He still holds the highest passer rating for any quarterback in the NFL. When he moved to the Chiefs in 1993, and people thought his career was over, he proved them all wrong by winning the Chiefs their first AFC Championship game. It's no wonder he was inducted into the Pro Football Hall of Fame in 2000.

Joe stood out on the field because he trained his body and mind. He practiced hard so that no matter how much pressure he faced, his body would always know exactly what to do. He trained his mind to see past fear and focus on the present. Because of all his hard work, the tension in the fourth quarter of his games never bothered him. Even when his team was losing and the pressure was on, he turned the game around time and again with complete calm.

Like Joe, you can train yourself to stay "cool" when things aren't looking good. When you face the challenges and do your best, you'll be surprised at the comebacks you can achieve.

THE IMMACULATE RECEPTION: WHEN THINGS DON'T GO TO PLAN

I n football history, no play has been discussed more than the "Immaculate Reception" from the Steelers vs. Raiders 1972 playoff game. Although "immaculate" means "perfect," this play was anything but flawless. It became famous because it *didn't* go to plan, and players like quarterback Terry Bradshaw and fullback Franco Harris had to adapt to a new plan quickly. But because they could confidently think on their feet, they led their team to victory and the greatest play in history.

BEFORE THE GAME

This playoff game was important for the Pittsburgh Steelers and Oakland Raiders for different reasons. The Raiders were regulars in the playoffs but missed them in 1971. Before that, they lost in the first playoff game for three consecutive years. This game was a chance for them to return to the playoffs and prove they could make it to the Super Bowl.

For the Steelers, this game meant something different. In 40 years of Steelers history, the team had never won a playoff game and had only made it to the playoffs once. The fact they made it so far in 1972 was a big deal to them, primarily thanks to Coach Chuck Noll and the team he'd been carefully putting together since he was hired in 1969. After Chuck became coach, the Steelers improved every year.

This game was also a rematch. The Steelers and Raiders played against each other in the first game of the season, and the Steelers won. The Raiders were eager to show they could beat the Steelers, while the Steelers had to defend their victory.

TERRY BRADSHAW'S THROW

For the first half of the game, both teams kept getting stopped partway down the field as the ball was passed back and forth. No one scored in the first half, which upped tensions in the second half. After an interception and two kicks by the Steelers' Roy Gerela, the Steelers gained six points while the Raiders still hadn't scored.

But the Raiders weren't done. Their quarterback, Kenny Stabler, ran 30 yards down the field for a touchdown, giving the Raiders the lead with a score of 7-6. If this had happened in the third quarter, the Steelers could have easily come back with another touchdown. The problem was that only one minute and 17 seconds remained in the game. The Steelers had little chance of getting another goal before the clock ran down.

They did their best, but with only 22 seconds left in the game, the Steelers were on their 40-yard line a long way from the end zone. Coach Chuck Noll called a play where the Steelers quarterback Terry Bradshaw would pass to rookie Barry

Pearson. Barry would then run down the field toward the end zone, although no one thought he would get far.

Even in the face of almost certain defeat, the Steelers got on the field and decided to do their best. The pressure was on. No doubt the team was nervous, wondering what would happen in the next 22 seconds. The Raiders were on their guard. To win, all they had to do was stop the Steelers from scoring. It would be difficult, if not impossible, to get past them.

But the Steelers knew the value of teamwork. Even those who weren't directly involved in the play were ready to do whatever they could to help their teammates.

No one could have guessed what happened when that play began. Terry Bradshaw instantly realized that things weren't going according to plan. Barry Pearson wasn't open, and the Raiders were closing in on Terry. At that moment, he could have panicked. He could have given up. But Terry had trained hard and was so confident in his abilities that he made a split-second decision. He threw the ball across the field to halfback John Fuqua, but Raiders safety Jack Tatum ran right into John as he tried to catch the ball.

It seemed like the end. The ball would drop, and the Steelers would lose their chance. That's when the impossible happened. The ball didn't fall; it bounced right off the Jack and John tangle and shot off.

FRANCO HARRIS' CATCH

No one was there to catch the ball—until Franco Harris zoomed in. The rookie fullback had been blocking but saw he was needed in a different place when Barry wasn't open to receiving

Terry's pass. Just like Terry, he could change plans at the last minute. He watched Terry throw the ball to John and saw the ball bounce off Jack. Franco ran straight toward it and caught the ball inches from the ground.

Franco ran for the end zone. It happened so quickly that the Raiders started cheering, thinking the ball had been dropped around John Fuqua. When everyone realized Franco was rushing down the field, the Raiders could do nothing. One player went in for a tackle, but Franco pushed him away and made it to the end zone with five seconds left. Franco's one moment of confidence gave his team the necessary victory.

Some fans were so excited they jumped out of the stands and ran onto the field before the Steelers' following kick could be made. Meanwhile, other fans were still trying to figure out what had happened. And so were the referees.

THE DEBATE

As everyone cheered, the game officials huddled together. Yes, the play was incredible, but there was a problem. The NFL rules at the time said that if the ball bounced off John Fuqua, the ball should not have continued in play, and the touchdown shouldn't have happened. However, if the ball bounced off Jack Tatum, the Raiders' safety, then the whole play was legal.

In the end, the head of the officials were called, and they debated what they had seen. In the 1970s, they didn't have instant replay, so it was hard to decide what had happened since it had gone by so fast. Jack Tatum stated the ball didn't touch him. Many on the Raiders team claimed they saw the ball bounce off John Fuqua. The Steelers team argued that the ball had only hit Jack Tatum.

Finally, the officials made the final call: touchdown for the Steelers!

However, even though the officials decided the Steelers had earned their touchdown, people still wonder about the Immaculate Reception to this day. With new technology, some have looked at footage of the play from different angles and said the ball bounced off of Jack, not John. In 2004, a physics professor did an experiment where he tried to recreate the throw to see which way the ball would have gone. He also said the ball must have hit Jack, making the Steelers' play valid.

THE LEGACY

After the win against the Raiders, the Steelers went on to the next playoff games. Although they lost before they could get to the Super Bowl, they were proud of their playoff victory. The 1972 season kickstarted the legendary Steelers dynasty, and they would win four Super Bowls in six years. The Immaculate Reception was the beginning of all the historic plays and records the Steelers would make over the next ten years.

However, no play ever beat the Immaculate Reception in popularity. It has been voted by fans, players, and the NFL multiple times as the greatest play in NFL history. Pittsburgh, Pennsylvania, is so proud of its Steelers that there are three monuments of the Immaculate Reception across the city.

Even though the play seems like it happened by chance, it ended in victory because the Steelers were willing to adapt when things didn't go to plan. When Terry couldn't throw to Barry, he did his best to get the ball down the field. Even though Franco wasn't supposed to be receiving, he ran forward, ready to help, and carried the ball down the field to complete the play.

In this play, the Steelers players learned that things don't always go how you think—both on the football field and in life. When things change unexpectedly, you have two choices. You can get upset and wish things were different or change along with the plan. Nobody on the Steelers team planned for that play to happen how it did, but instead of complaining, they did their best anyway and completed the best play in NFL history.

Change is hard, but you can learn to adapt. The next time a plan changes, try going along with it. Maybe the path you end up on will be even more rewarding than the one you planned for.

ANTHONY MUÑOZ:
THE MAN WHO WOULDN'T GIVE UP

A LEGEND ALMOST MISSED

When Anthony Muñoz was on the field, he grabbed everyone's attention. He never said much, but his plays said it all. He could stop a player on the opposite team just by letting them run into him. He could mow down quarterbacks, running backs, and linemen alike, no matter their size.

There's never been another football player like Anthony, powerful both on the field and when facing life's challenges. He's known as the best offensive lineman the NFL has ever had.

But, as amazing as he was, Anthony almost didn't make it to the NFL draft. He would never have become the legend we know today if he hadn't persevered, which means to keep going when life gets tough. Perseverance might be the most important thing that Anthony Muñoz learned.

Anthony's life seemed perfect during and after his victorious football career, but it wasn't always that way. Anthony had a loving mom as a child but missed his dad. It was hard for him to grow up with only one parent. Anthony faced this challenge and learned how to persevere from his mom, who raised Anthony and his four siblings on her own. She looked and acted tough but loved her children and always cheered on Anthony throughout his football career.

Anthony's mom told him he should start playing on sports teams at five years old. Anthony looked much older than he was, so he played with kids twice his age. As a boy, his favorite sport was baseball; he played it on any team whenever he could. He played on so many local baseball teams that sometimes two of his teams would play each other, and they would argue over who got to have him!

COLLEGE INJURIES

Anthony continued playing baseball throughout his school years, but in high school, people suggested he play football. He was big and strong, the perfect build for a great football player. So, after he graduated, Anthony accepted a football scholarship to Southern California University (SCU), though he played baseball while he was there, too.

His college years didn't go as planned. While the SCU Trojans won a bowl game all four years that Anthony played with them, he only got to be in two. In Anthony's first season, he was injured and kept getting hurt over the next four years. These injuries stopped him from playing many games, but he got on the field whenever possible. If he knew how to do one thing, it was to persevere.

Even though Anthony's senior year was extremely short, it will always be remembered. In the very first game of the season, Anthony got a bad knee injury that needed surgery. He was out for the rest of the season—or, at least, he should have been. Everyone expected Anthony to sit out for the rest of the year, but the Trojans made it to the Rose Bowl for their final game, and Anthony wanted to be there. To everyone's surprise, he showed up and played without getting injured again. Anthony's coach was so impressed that he said this about him afterward: "He played the whole ball game, he didn't get hurt, and we won. To me, that's a perfect game. That's one of the greatest things I've ever seen happen."

It's a good thing Anthony decided to play in the Rose Bowl because someone very special was watching him from the stands. Paul Brown, founder and manager of the Cincinnati Bengals, was just as impressed as Anthony's coach. He couldn't believe he'd found such an incredible player right under his nose. Anthony was just what he needed for his team.

DOUBTS AND VICTORIES

Paul Brown didn't waste any time. He picked Anthony third in the NFL draft, and Anthony became a Bengal. Many didn't think this was a good idea because Anthony's injuries kept him from playing so often. He'd missed out on most of his college games because of them. But Paul Brown had seen Anthony play, and he saw in him the heart and soul of a legendary football player. Anthony immediately became a starter, which rarely happens in a player's rookie season.

Anthony's coaches and teammates soon realized that Anthony differed from most other players. One thing was different: his size. Anthony was six and a half feet tall and around 280 pounds when he was drafted, making him one of the biggest players on his team. As an offensive lineman, this was a good thing for him. He could easily plow through the opposing team, sometimes lifting players off the ground.

Anthony was different in other ways, too. It's normal for football players to get angry during a game; maybe they made a mistake, or perhaps they don't like the referee's call. However, Anthony never got angry on the field. Most players never heard him speak at all. Anthony didn't waste his energy on getting upset when something terrible happened. He had learned the lesson of perseverance first from his mom and then from getting injured in college. Anthony knew that when he couldn't change the situation, all he could do was keep going and playing his best.

That was his attitude in every game. Instead of getting angry, Anthony focused. Instead of talking trash about the other team, he said he was sorry when he accidentally hurt someone.

Anthony was also careful. He had been injured so many times that he knew taking care of his body was important. He had to exercise to stay in shape, but he kept those exercises simple. His care paid off! Anthony stayed with the Bengals for 12 seasons and only missed three games.

AN UNFORGETTABLE PLAYER

Anthony was such a great football player that recording his best games, records, and awards would take too many pages. However, Anthony earned some titles that show how special he was to his teammates, his coaches, and NFL fans across the country. Over his 13-year football career, he was chosen to be an All-Pro offensive lineman 11 times and selected as Offensive Lineman of the Year six times. In The Top 100: NFL's Greatest Players, he was ranked the twelfth greatest player in NFL history—the highest-ranked offensive lineman on that list. In 1998, Anthony received the greatest honor for any football player by being accepted into the Pro Football Hall of Fame. Only the best of the best make it in there!

Anthony Muñoz is, without a doubt, one of the greatest football players of all time. His career was almost very different, though. If he had let his knee injury stop him from going to the Rose Bowl in his senior year of college, he wouldn't have been spotted by Paul Brown and drafted by the Bengals. He might not have even made it to pro football, and he might not be the legend we know him as today.

But Anthony persevered. No matter what came his way, he kept going. He kept playing. He kept living the life he loved, even when it was hard.

Sometimes, life doesn't happen the way you expect it to. Maybe, just like Anthony, you're already facing challenges. If you choose to persevere, you can expect amazing things ahead. You never know when your "Rose Bowl moment" is right around the corner, so keep going!

JERRY RICE:
AN UNLIKELY LEGEND

IMAGINING A BETTER FUTURE

If you saw Jerry Rice when he was young, helping his father lay bricks to build houses, picking crops in the fields to help feed his family, and running several miles home from school because he didn't have a ride, you probably wouldn't imagine he would one day become known to many as "the greatest player in NFL history."

Growing up wasn't always easy for Jerry. His family struggled to earn enough money to live, so from a young age, Jerry and his seven siblings were expected to help out in any way they could. When he wasn't in school, Jerry helped his dad at work or searched around his hometown of Crawford, Mississippi for free food. This didn't leave him much time to hang out with friends, and even if he could, something as simple as going to the movies was too much for his family to afford.

Jerry faced many challenges. He could have let them affect his positive attitude, but instead, he looked past the hard times and promised to create a better future for himself and his family. At first, he didn't know what that future would look like, but it became more apparent when Jerry got to high school.

That was when he realized helping his dad lay bricks had strengthened him. Picking food for his family taught him to be quick in mind and feet. Running home from school helped him to practice running so quickly that he was eventually brought onto his high school football team as an extraordinary wide receiver. It wasn't playing football that helped Jerry to become a great athlete—it was a lot of hard work and practice.

BECOMING A PRO

When Jerry Rice made it to the NFL after college, he had to pass a challenging test: the 40-yard dash. In this test, players who want to be in the NFL must run 40 yards as fast as possible. The faster the run, the higher the score. Jerry completed the dash in 4.7 seconds, and while that may sound fast, it was on the slower end for a football player, and especially for a wide receiver. Jerry's speed didn't look great, but he decided not to focus on what he *couldn't* do. Instead, he looked beyond the hardships to see what was possible, just like when he was little. He knew that he had a chance to learn and grow stronger from every challenging situation.

Jerry soon discovered he didn't have to be fast as long as he could be precise. He studied playbooks constantly to understand how he and his teammates would move on the field during a game. Then, he designed a workout routine so crazy that other NFL players tried it with him and got sick before the first day was even over.

The most famous part of his workout was called "The Hill." Jerry would run up a steep 2.5-mile hill every day during the offseason. That's about 2500 steps! Running up hills is difficult because your body works extra hard to move upward *and* forward while gravity pulls you down.

Even though this exercise wasn't easy, it gave Jerry the ability to get a quick running start. Because of his weight training, he became very strong and could hold onto the football on the field, even when the other team tried to take it from him or stop him from jumping and grabbing it.

His practice and hard work—mainly off the field—paid off. People noticed the difference between Jerry Rice and all the other NFL players. It wasn't because Jerry was special. It wasn't because he knew a magic secret about playing football. It was just because he understood that to become great, he had to practice, work hard, and learn from every challenge.

JERRY'S BIGGEST GAME

Although Jerry played for a few different NFL teams throughout his career, he's most known for playing with the San Francisco 49ers for 15 years. He was drafted in 1985 right out of college. His first season was so stunning that Pat Summerall, a CBS announcer, Pat Summerall, said, "When this guy is finished, he'll be considered one of the greatest wide receivers to ever play this game." By the end of his rookie season, Jerry had 49 catches, 927 yards, and three receiving touchdowns. He was even named NFC Offensive Rookie of the Year.

But one of Jerry's crowning achievements came in Super Bowl XXIII against the Cincinnati Bengals in 1989. While the 49ers were doing well, their ten-win and six-loss season wasn't as good as it had been. And this wasn't the first time the 49ers had met the Bengals either; they had faced off in Super Bowl XVI six years before. It was time for a rematch.

The game started slow; it was clear that the two teams were well-matched. Nobody scored until the third quarter when the teams were tied from field goals. But then, a touchdown was made; the Bengals scored.

The game rolled into the fourth quarter and the 49ers were nervous. But when the big lights came on, Jerry Rice performed his best because he'd put in hours of practice. From a difficult childhood that made him courageous and creative to the crazy practice routine that gave him speed and strength, Jerry knew he was prepared for this moment.

Things weren't looking too good at the start of the fourth quarter. But then, out of nowhere, Jerry Rice streaked down the field to catch a 14-yard touchdown! The score was now tied 13-13.

The stands erupted with applause, but the game wasn't over yet. The Bengals soon got back in the lead with only three minutes and 20 seconds left. Even though the clock was ticking closer to the end of the game, Jerry plowed down the field, making catch after catch until the 49ers ended up at the 10-yard line with only 34 seconds left. The Bengals led 16-13. This was the 49er's last chance.

Touchdown! In an amazing display of teamwork, the winning catch went to another wide receiver, John Taylor. However, the ball would have never gotten down the field without Jerry's persistence. Jerry was so important to winning the game that he became the 49ers Super Bowl MVP. He ended the game with 11 receptions, 215 yards, and a touchdown.

THE LEGACY

With a final score of 20-16, the 49ers became the first NFC team to win three Super Bowls. Jerry Rice solidified his place in history and made incredible plays until he retired in 2006. The 49ers were so proud of their all-star player that even though Jerry had gone on to play for other teams, the 49ers signed him for a one-day contract so that he could retire on the same team he'd started with, the team that made his career, and the team he loved the most. Since retiring, Jerry has won many awards and honors and is often recognized as one of the NFL's greatest players.

Jerry's story reminds us that there is always something to be gained, even in the face of challenges. Every hardship and tough situation has the potential to shape us into stronger and wiser people. Through these times, we can discover our true potential and learn lessons that will stay with us for a lifetime.

Jerry Rice once talked about the "secret" to his success, which is something anyone can do—even you! "Today I will do what others won't so tomorrow I can do what others can't." This means that Jerry put in hard work and practice every day because he knew it would pay off the next day. Practice is hard. "Hard work" is called "hard" for a reason! But if you keep going, keep practicing, and use every situation to grow stronger, you can be just like Jerry Rice and do the impossible.

RUSSELL WILSON: WHAT'S MORE IMPORTANT THAN FOOTBALL?

LEARNING FROM FAMILY

Russell Wilson was a born athlete. Even though he proved good at football, baseball, and basketball from a young age, his dad always taught him that some things were more important than football. He told Russell that taking care of himself and staying professional on and off the field was important. Most of all, he taught Russell to have a "Why not you?" attitude. He told his son that anything was possible if he believed in himself and put his mind to it. As a young boy, Russell took his dad's lessons to heart and believed he would win the Super Bowl one day. His dad even made him practice his winning speech.

Meanwhile, Russell's older brother Harry taught him always to do his best and never give up. As a kid, Russell could never beat Harry in a game. He would get frustrated and go inside to complain to his mom. She always asked Russell if he would quit, and instead of giving up, Russell would go back outside and try to beat Harry. Even though he lost every time, he kept playing because the best part wasn't winning—it was having fun with his brother.

Russell's mom and dad showed him that faith and kindness were important parts of life. From a young age, when Russell was upset, he counted on his faith to get him through hard times. This would continue to be an important part of his life that kept him positive through the ups and downs of his football career.

Russell took his family's lessons with him when he started playing football on a team in sixth grade. He loved nothing more than getting out there on the field but also knew that school was important. When he struggled with a class, he asked his friends to help him with his homework. By simply studying and asking for help when needed, Russell kept his grades up while staying dedicated to football throughout middle and high school.

BECOMING AN ALL-STAR QUARTERBACK

Russell's reputation for working hard wasn't the only thing that got him on the high school football team. In tenth grade, Russell competed for quarterback with a boy who was a grade ahead of him and several inches taller. The odds were stacked against Russell, but he won, becoming his team's quarterback. As a senior, Russell made it into the famous magazine *Sports Illustrated* for helping his team win the state championship.

In 2008, Russell made a name for himself when he began his football career with the Wolfpack of North Carolina State

University. Though Russell initially traded off the quarterback position with two other players older than him, after his fifth week, Russell became the team's only quarterback. In 2010, his third and final year on the team, Russell had a record of 274.1 passing yards per game and 307.5 total offensive yards per game, the highest numbers in the Atlantic Coast Conference (ACC). He was a big part of the Wolfpack's nine-win-four-loss season and was named the second choice for ACC Football Player of the Year.

Russell transferred to the Wisconsin Badgers team for his final year in college football. During the season, Russell led his team to several wins, even against the undefeated Nebraska Cornhuskers. He had 33 passing touchdowns by the end of the season, which broke the previous Badgers record, and was awarded multiple titles and honors.

THE FIRST PRO SEASONS

In 2012, the Seattle Seahawks drafted Russell. Many didn't think this was a good choice for the Seahawks, as Russell was fresh out of college and a little short for a quarterback. They would soon be proven wrong.

Before the season began, Russell was in a familiar situation: his coach had him compete with other players to become the team's starting quarterback. Once again, Russell won. As a rookie, he became the starting quarterback for the Seahawks. Russell did so well in his first season that he broke even more records. For example, he ended the season ranked fourth in the NFL's passer rating, beating the previous rookie record.

Russell's excellent abilities helped him and his team make it to the Super Bowl the following year. Russell was ready for it—he had his speech prepared, after all! With 206 yards and two touchdowns, Russell was a big part of the 43-8 victory over the Denver Broncos. It was the first time the Seahawks won the Super Bowl.

Russell's dedication didn't stop there. He kept playing his best and led the Seahawks to the Super Bowl again next year. It was the first time a winning team had returned in ten years. And with that game, Russell also broke another record. No starting quarterback had ever been to the Super Bowl twice within their first three seasons.

BEST QUARTERBACK PERFORMANCE

Russell had many great performances throughout his career, but one of the best was in the 2018 Seahawks vs. Detroit Lions game. It wasn't because of how many yards Russell threw or how many big-time throws he made, but because of how his passes were graded. Yes, football players get graded, too. It doesn't matter how many times they throw the ball, but how good those throws are. When Russell threw straight and true, his score went up. So, even though he had the fewest passes of the season in the Lions game, they all got nearly perfect scores because they were thrown so well. Only one of Russell's throws was slightly off, and even that one made a touchdown.

During the game, the Lions could only make two touchdowns, one at the beginning and another at the end. Meanwhile, Russell's throws made three touchdowns in the second quarter. The Seahawks won easily, 28-14. Russell finished the game with an average of 14.6 yards per attempt and 11.6 yards of target depth—much higher than the NFL quarterback average.

Overall, Russell was rated so high in his performance (98 out of 100!) that he broke the record for the best quarterback grade in all the NFL for 2018. He finished the game with 248 yards along with his 17 throws, and though many quarterbacks had higher numbers than that, none of them could throw as well as Russell.

Russell continued to play for the Seahawks until 2021, breaking records, leading as team captain, and helping his team win multiple victories. His teammates voted for him to earn numerous awards and honors, the most important being the Walter Payton Man of the Year award.

WHAT'S MOST IMPORTANT

The Walter Payton Man of the Year award is one of the most significant and important awards in the NFL because it's not just about how well someone plays on the field. You might think that's a bit strange, but Russell Wilson and many other athletes understand that being a good person is more important than being a good athlete. So, the Walter Payton Man of the Year award is voted on by NFL players and is given to the athlete who shows excellence on *and* off the field.

This award proved that while Russell's amazing records and wins were important, he loved helping people and giving back to his community even more than football. Russell never forgot the lessons his family taught him about all the things more important than football: faith, confidence, never giving up, and kindness.

In 2014, Russell started the Why Not You Foundation with his wife. Their goal is to help kids in need and encourage them to believe in themselves, just like Russell's dad taught him as a kid.

Through this foundation, Russell has provided millions of meals for needy families, given kids access to good schools, and funded cancer research. He also worked closely with the Seattle Children's Hospital for many years and met with kids in need nationwide.

Russell was a popular person both on and off the field. His teammates continuously voted for him to earn multiple awards and honors, and it's not because they thought he was the coolest or best NFL player (although he was very good). His teammates voted him team captain eight years in a row because they recognized he had a huge heart and looked after others.

Even though our talents are important, loving others is even more important. Doing your best to help your friends, family, and community whenever possible makes you and others feel great. You never know how much good even a small act of kindness can do! It can be as simple as holding the door for your friend or sharing a game with one of your siblings.

Just like Russell Wilson, you can be known for the strength of your heart; the first step is simply being kind.

CONCLUSION

Did you know you can be just as amazing as all the athletes you read about?

None of these incredible football players had "special powers" that made them better than anyone else. They might have accomplished some crazy things, but underneath, they were everyday people who chose to make themselves extraordinary. If they can do it, so can you.

The secret is that each of these men embraced who they were and lived life on and off the field using their strengths. J. J. Watt worked hard to become a strong player but also used his smaller size to his advantage to be quick on his feet. Jerry Rice's constant determination meant he always brought his best to the field. Patrick Mahomes' out-of-the-box helped him come up with wild throws that other teams wouldn't see coming. Joe Montana used his ability to stay calm under pressure to make several comebacks for his team.

What are your skills? Maybe you're great at making people smile. Perhaps you have a good memory. Maybe you're tidy and organized. No matter how ordinary your strengths may seem, you can turn them into something extraordinary, just like all these fantastic athletes did. Whether you grow up as a football player, astronaut, doctor, teacher, or anything else, you can use your gifts to give your best every day. When you embrace who you are and let your strengths shine, you'll be on your way to notable achievements like the ones you read about in this book.

You don't need to wait until you grow up to use these unique gifts. You can make the world a better place little by little, whether by helping your friend through a challenging time or creating a work of art for someone you love. Every day counts. Every little action means something to someone.

So, read these stories again and again to discover new ways to show confidence, kindness, perseverance, and all the other skills these players showed. Never forget that, just like your favorite athletes, you are extraordinary. Don't be afraid to love who you are and show off your unique talents, skills, and strengths every day.

Maybe one day, a book will tell your story, too.

FUN FOOTBALL FACTS

GENERAL FACTS

★ Football is the most popular sport in the United States.

★ NFL stands for National Football League.

★ Football is more technically known as "gridiron football" or "American football," as most other countries refer to soccer as football.

★ The average salary for an NFL player is $860,000.

★ The New York Jets beat the Philadelphia Eagles for the first time in 2023. Before that, the Jets lost to the Eagles 12 times.

★ The company Wilson has been making the NFL's footballs for over 70 years.

★ NFL games have bigger audiences on average than any other sports league worldwide.

★ Only one state, Texas, uses college football rules for high school programs, following the National Collegiate Athletic Association (NCAA) standards.

★ The Wilson Football Factory produces over 700,000 footballs annually for the United States.

★ There are 32 teams in the NFL.

★ The only team to play their home games in New York is the Buffalo Bills; the New York Giants and New York Jets play in New Jersey.

★ The NFL season lasts 17 weeks, and 256 combined games are played throughout the league.

★ MetLife Stadium in New Jersey is the largest NFL stadium in the country, with 82,500 seats. The New York Giants and New York Jets share MetLife Stadium and each season, they switch who gets to play there for home games.

★ When the NFL first started in 1920, it had only ten teams. Two of those teams remain today: the Arizona Cardinals and Chicago Bears.

★ The NFL draft has seven rounds.

★ Florida has three NFL teams: the Tampa Bay Buccaneers, the Miami Dolphins, and the Jacksonville Jaguars.

★ The 32 teams in the NFL come from 23 different states across the United States.

★ Before moving to Baltimore, the Ravens were initially based in Cleveland, Ohio.

* Ten minutes after a 1976 playoff game between the Pittsburgh Steelers and Indianapolis Colts at Memorial Stadium, a small plane crashed into the stadium. Fortunately, no one was hurt.

THE GAME

* A standard football field is 360 feet long and 160 feet wide, 1.32 acres.

* A football game lasts 60 minutes with four quarters, each divided into 15 minutes. However, the game lasts much longer with time outs, halftime, overtime, and clock stops for reasons like a ball going out of bounds.

* Each football team can only have 11 players on the field at a time. Since players switch out often, NFL teams are allowed to have 53 players on their active roster.

* End zones are 10 yards long. Once a player gets into this area with the football by running or catching a pass, they win a six-point touchdown.

* Each team is allowed three timeouts per half. They can be called by players or the coach and are used for various reasons. Sometimes, they may simply want to stop the clock close to the end of a game or quarter, or the coach might want to stop their team's current play.

* A field goal is worth three points. A team can attempt a field goal on any down, but if they miss, the opposing team takes possession of the ball.

★ When a player drops the football after running with it, it's a fumble. Most often, the other team picks up the ball.

★ When a pass is accidentally thrown to the other team, it's called an interception.

RECORDS

★ The Chicago Bears, New England Patriots, and Miami Dolphins are the only NFL teams to complete a perfect regular season. However, only the Dolphins had a perfect season, including the postseason, when they went 17-0-0 in 1972.

★ The longest-ever NFL game was played between the Miami Dolphins and the Kansas City Chiefs in 1971. It lasted almost 83 minutes.

★ The Green Bay Packers is the oldest NFL team with the same name and plays in the same location. It was formed in 1919 in Green Bay, Wisconsin.

★ The New England Patriots hold the longest winning streak in the NFL, 21 games.

★ The record for most points in a college game goes to Georgia Tech, who finished the game with a score of 222-0 in 1916.

★ The Green Bay Packers have so many fans that they have the longest waitlist for season tickets in the entire NFL. Over 100,000 people are on the list every year, and most won't be able to get the tickets during their lifetime, even if they're on the list every year.

★ The Tampa Bay Buccaneers had the longest losing streak in NFL history in the 1976-77 season of 26 games.

★ Mark Moseley is the only kicker who has ever won the NFL's MVP.

★ The Arizona Cardinals is the oldest continuous pro football team. It was formed in 1898 as the Morgan Athletic Club.

★ Sarah Thomas became the NFL's first official female referee in 2015.

★ In 1943, Sammy Baugh played quarterback, defense back, and punter because of roster depletions during World War II. In one game, he threw four touchdown passes, had an 81-yard punt, and caught four interceptions, playing all three of his positions in one game.

★ Gale Sayers was 34 when he was inducted into the Pro Football Hall of Fame in 1977, making him the youngest player ever to be inducted.

★ Two different times, the Detroit Lions went 30 years without winning a playoff game.

★ Receiver Brett Favre of the Green Bay Packers threw his first-ever NFL pass to himself. The ball bounced off an opposing player's helmet and returned to him.

★ The New England Patriots have won the most NFL playoff games (37).

★ The longest college football game was played between Kentucky and Arkansas in 2003. The game was almost four hours long and had seven overtime periods.

★ The record for career passing yards belongs to Tom Brady, who passed 89,214 yards (over 50 miles) across his 23-season career.

★ The most valuable NFL team is the Dallas Cowboys, worth almost $8 billion.

★ The leading scorer in the history of the NFL is New England Patriots and Indianapolis Colts placekicker Adam Vinatieri, who scored 2,673 points throughout his career.

★ San Diego Chargers running back LaDainian Tomlinson holds the record for most touchdowns in a season. In 2006, he recorded 31 touchdowns.

★ In 2013, Denver Broncos quarterback Peyton Manning broke the record for most passing yards in a season with 5,477 yards.

★ Wide receiver Jerry Rice of the San Francisco 49ers holds the record for the most touchdowns in a career (208).

★ Sprinter and split-end Bob Hayes is the only man in history to have an Olympic gold medal and a Super Bowl ring. He won two Olympic gold medals at the 1964 Olympic Summer Games and helped the Dallas Cowboys win their first Super Bowl in 1972.

★ Three teams have never gotten the number one pick in the NFL draft: the Denver Broncos, Seattle Seahawks, and Baltimore Ravens. This is partially a good thing, as the first pick goes to the team with the worst season record. However, the draft picks were initially random, and none of these three teams got picked.

★ Tom Brady is the richest football player in history, having earned over $300 million throughout his 23 seasons in the NFL.

THE SUPER BOWL

★ Twelve NFL teams have never won the Super Bowl.

★ The Super Bowl was initially called the NFL-AFL Championship Game until Kansas City Chiefs owner Lamar Hunt coined the term "Super Bowl."

★ Out of the 20 most viewed television broadcasts in the United States, 19 are Super Bowls.

★ About 115 million people watch the Super Bowl every year.

★ Four NFL teams have never appeared at the Super Bowl: the Detroit Lions, Jacksonville Jaguars, Cleveland Browns, and Houston Texans.

★ Miami has hosted the Super Bowl more times than any other team.

★ Playing a 30-second commercial during the Super Bowl costs companies several million dollars.

- ★ The first Super Bowl tickets cost $12; this was the only Super Bowl that didn't sell out. Today, each ticket costs thousands of dollars, and getting one is nearly impossible.

- ★ The Green Bay Packers won the first Super Bowl in 1967.

- ★ Super Bowl XLIX in 2015 was the most-watched Super Bowl game ever, with 114.4 million viewers.

- ★ From 1982-1995, the San Francisco 49ers won five Super Bowls. This is mainly due to some legendary players on the team at the time, such as Jerry Rice, Joe Montana, Steve Young, and Ronnie Lott.

- ★ The Pittsburgh Steelers and the New England Patriots hold the record for the most Super Bowl wins (6).

- ★ The trophy that Super Bowl champions win is called the Vince Lombardi trophy. It's named after the coach of the Green Bay Packers, who won the first two Super Bowls.

- ★ Peyton and Eli Manning, both quarterbacks in the NFL, were the only brothers to win Super Bowl MVP, Peyton in 2007 and Eli in 2012.

- ★ The Buffalo Bills played in four Super Bowls from 1990 to 1993 and lost each time.

- ★ The Lombardi Trophy weighs seven pounds.

- ★ Linebacker Chuck Howley was the first non-quarterback to win the Super Bowl MVP award and the only MVP winner from the losing team. He intercepted two passes and forced a fumble but refused to accept his trophy because he was so upset about the Dallas Cowboys' loss.

HISTORY

★ American football was born of a combination of soccer and rugby.

★ Jay Berwanger was the first player in an NFL draft in 1939.

★ In the early 1900s, President Theodore Roosevelt said he would ban football nationwide unless the rules were changed so players were safer.

★ NFL players didn't have to wear helmets until 1943.

★ The first televised pro football game was only watched by about 500 households in 1939.

★ The NFL was founded in 1920 and was initially called the American Professional Football Association.

★ The first football game took place in 1869 between Rutgers and Princeton.

★ Glenn Scobey "Pop" Warner created several football practices and plays still in use today. His contributions to football are so famous that there is a popular youth football program named "Pop Warner" after him.

REVIEW

As a children's book author, it would not only be a great help but also a joy for me if you could leave an honest review on Amazon.

I believe that these types of books play a crucial role in nurturing children's character, boosting their self-confidence, enhancing their relationships with friends and family, and encouraging them to be the best version of themselves, all while bringing them happiness.

I hope we can share many more stories together!

Here's the QR code for the review.

REFERENCES

If you want to check the references of the stories, as well as the facts, you can do so by scanning these two QR codes!

Football stories references   *Football facts references*

Made in the USA
Las Vegas, NV
09 November 2024

10943544R00069